NATURE'S CHILDREN™

FALCONS

by Katie Marsico

Children's Press®

An Imprint of Scholastic Inc.
New York Toronto London Auckland Sydney
Mexico City New Delhi Hong Kong
Danbury, Connecticut

Content Consultant
Dr. Stephen S. Ditchkoff
Professor of Wildlife Sciences
Auburn University
Auburn, Alabama

Photographs ©: age fotostock/John Hawkins: 28; Alamy Images: 8
(Jerome Murray), 22, 23 (Oyvind Martinsen); Christopher Jimenez:
26, 27; Dreamstime: 5 bottom, 38, 39 (Arvidas Saladauskas), 2
background, 3 background, 44 background, 45 background (Egidijus
Mika), 14, 15 (Lukas Blazek), 20 (Steve Liptrot), 5 top, 19 (Willi Van
Boven); Science Source: 24, 25 (Jim Zipp), 40, 41 (Peter Skinner);
Shutterstock, Inc.: 16 (Brian Lasenby), 1, 7 (Nick Biemans), 36, 37
(Tracy Starr); Superstock, Inc.: 2, 3, 10, 11, 46 (Animals Animals),
30, 31 (Biosphoto), cover (FLPA), 34, 35 (Minden Pictures), 4, 5
background, 12, 32, 33 (NHPA).

Library of Congress Cataloging-in-Publication Data
Marsico, Katie, 1980– author.
  Falcons / by Katie Marsico.
      pages cm. — (Nature's children)
  Summary: "This book details the life and habits of falcons."—
Provided by publisher.
  Audience: Ages 9–12.
  Audience: Grades 4 to 6.
  Includes bibliographical references and index.
  ISBN 978-0-531-21168-7 (library binding) —
ISBN 978-0-531-21187-8 (pbk.)
1. Falcons—Juvenile literature. I. Title. II. Series: Nature's children
(New York, N.Y.)
  QL696.F34M343 2015
  598.9'6—dc23
2014029911

All rights reserved. Published in 2015 by Children's Press, an imprint
of Scholastic Inc.

Printed in China 62
SCHOLASTIC, CHILDREN'S PRESS, and associated logos are
trademarks and/or registered trademarks of Scholastic Inc.

1 2 3 4 5 6 7 8 9 10 R 24 23 22 21 20 19 18 17 16 15

Falcons

Class	Aves
Order	Falconiformes
Family	Falconidae
Subfamilies	Falconinae and Polyborinae
Genera	Around 11 genera
Species	Around 60 species
World distribution	Most parts of the world, except for Antarctica and certain portions of the Arctic
Habitats	Deserts, tundras, grasslands, savannas, forests, mountains, coastal areas, wetlands, lakeshores, and farmland; sometimes found in more developed locations such as towns and cities
Distinctive physical characteristics	A bony ridge above the eyeballs; three pairs of eyelids; ear holes positioned behind and underneath the eyes; a hooked beak; large, forward-facing eyes; short, pointed wings; short neck and tail; a streamlined body; sharp, curved talons
Habits	Diurnal; hunts prey; tends to be territorial and solitary; typically monogamous, reproducing about once a year
Diet	Insects, birds, small mammals and reptiles; occasionally scavenges rotting fruit and carrion

FALCONS

Contents

CHAPTER 1
6 Flying Fast and Fierce

CHAPTER 2
13 Amazing Adaptations

CHAPTER 3
26 A Falcon's Life Cycle

CHAPTER 4
33 Past and Present Identity

CHAPTER 5
38 The Future for Falcons

42 Words to Know
44 Habitat Map
46 Find Out More
47 Index
48 About the Author

Flying Fast and Fierce

The morning sun beats down on a noise-filled **mudflat** along California's Pacific coast. The air hums with the quacks and caws of seagulls and other shorebirds. Suddenly their chorus grows shriller. The noise is accompanied by an excited fluttering of wings.

The reason for the birds' panic is soon made clear. Watching from high among the seaside cliffs, a sharp-eyed peregrine falcon has spied its next meal. This skilled and speedy hunter dives toward an unlucky gull hovering above the mudflat. Both birds are still in flight when the falcon uses its powerful **talons** and sharp beak to overtake its screeching **prey**.

Falcons are a **family** of **diurnal** raptors, or **predatory** birds that tend to hunt in daylight. As they dive, falcons often reach remarkable speeds. Peregrines are considered the fastest birds on Earth. They can dive up to 200 miles (322 kilometers) per hour.

Falcons often spot prey from a great distance and swoop in for the kill.

Where Falcons Are Found

Falcons are found almost everywhere except Antarctica and certain parts of the Arctic. The broadest range of **species** exists in South America and Africa. These raptors live in a wide variety of **habitats**, including deserts, **tundras**, grasslands, **savannas**, mountains, and forests. They also live in coastal areas and wetlands, at lakeshores, and on farmlands. Some species have **adapted** to more developed **environments** as well. It is not uncommon for peregrines to perch along bridges and building ledges in towns and cities.

Falcons don't typically build their own nests out of sticks and leaves. Instead, some use old nests made by other birds. Certain species also dig shallow depressions called scrapes in cliffs or along the ground. Some falcons spend time in caves and tree holes, too.

Falcons don't necessarily stay in the same area all year long. Some **migrate** to warmer locations as the seasons change. Depending on where a falcon lives, it can be challenging for it to find food once winter sets in.

Tree holes make a perfect home for certain species of falcon.

Physical Features

There are at least 60 species of falcons. Each has unique characteristics. While the majority of these raptors are small- to medium-sized birds, the Seychelles kestrel is the tiniest. Its wingspan measures just 16 to 18 inches (41 to 46 centimeters) in length. Seychelles kestrels weigh 2.6 to 3.1 ounces (74 to 88 grams). Meanwhile, gyrfalcons are the largest species of falcon. Their wingspan stretches more than 4 feet (1.2 meters), and they weigh 1.8 to 4.6 pounds (0.8 to 2 kilograms).

Most falcons have large brown eyes and a hooked beak. Each of their two feet has four toes that end in sharp talons. Feathers cover most of their body. They are usually various shades of brown, black, gray, or white. Sometimes a falcon's feathers are marked by stripes or spots as well.

Adult male
6 ft. (1.8 m)

Gyrfalcon
wingspan 4 ft. (1.2 m)

Seychelles kestrel
wingspan 18 in. (46 cm)

On average, female gyrfalcons are about twice the size of males.

CHAPTER 2

Amazing Adaptations

Other than eagles, large owls, and occasionally wolves, falcons face few natural predators. They hunt a wide range of animals, including insects, birds, and small **mammals** and **reptiles**. Certain species also eat rotting fruit and **carrion**.

Falcons eat often to support their speedy **metabolism**, which in turn creates a steady supply of energy. This helps them fly fast and hunt efficiently. Like other diurnal raptors, falcons have a crop in their throat. This is a pouch where food is stored before it is digested. A falcon's crop allows it to eat large amounts of food in a short period of time. Falcons also have high levels of stomach acid. The acid makes it easier for falcons to digest prey with small, pointy bones.

FUN FACT! Because meat is high in water content, diurnal raptors do not need to drink much water.

Several species of falcon feed on mice.

A Strong, Streamlined Body

Many falcons have physical features that help them soar with speed. A large keel is one such feature. The keel is a ridge along a bird's breastbone that is attached to the muscles involved in flight. The size of a falcon's keel allows it to support very powerful chest muscles.

Falcons have short, pointed wings and a short neck and tail. Along with slim, firm feathers positioned closely together, these qualities give falcons a streamlined shape. This means they can move swiftly and smoothly through the air.

Falcons such as peregrines sometimes kill prey on the fly and simply carry off their meal. In other situations, they stun or injure an animal and then retrieve it after it falls to the ground. These attacks depend on quick, precise movements. Long, drawn-out struggles increase the odds of prey escaping or falcons being injured.

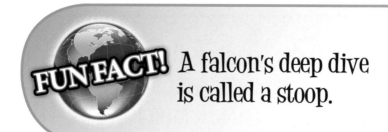

FUN FACT! A falcon's deep dive is called a stoop.

A falcon's wide, powerful chest makes it a strong flyer.

Feet, Toes, and Talons

Falcons use their sharp, curved talons to snatch up prey. Sometimes they also clench their claws together the same way people ball up their hands to make fists. Their feet and talons then become weapons they can use to strike and stun prey.

A falcon's foot muscles and claws allow it to steer during steep dives. In addition, they help these birds grip surfaces when landing. A falcon's scale-covered feet and toes are also useful for carving out scrapes.

Different species have slightly different feet and talons. For example, falcons that feed mainly on other birds tend to have longer toes. This helps them reach through feathers to more firmly grip their prey. Meanwhile, caracaras usually have strong, sturdy legs and feet. This is because they often hunt prey that is on the ground instead of snatching it from the air. As a result, they sometimes need to chase after their meals on foot.

A caracara is better suited to ground movement than most other falcons.

The Benefits of a Beak

A falcon's sharp, hooked beak plays a huge role in both its hunting and eating. In many cases, the animals that falcons eat are too large to be swallowed whole. Instead, a falcon uses its beak to tear off chunks of skin, fur, and feathers. It can then tear its meal into smaller pieces that are easier to digest.

A falcon's tomial tooth is another important feature. This small, triangular tooth is located in the upper half of the bird's beak. It is a powerful and deadly weapon that helps raptors kill their prey faster. When a falcon clamps its beak down, the tomial tooth slices through a target's spine. Such a bite is either crippling or fatal. As a result, falcons are able to spend more time eating and less time involved in a struggle.

A falcon's beak is capable of ripping past an animal's fur, feathers, or skin to reach the meat inside.

Impressive Eyesight

Falcons depend on their sharp eyesight to spot prey from more than 1.9 miles (3 km) away. Like people, they have forward-facing eyes that allow for binocular vision. This means there is some overlap between what their left and right eyes are viewing at any given moment.

Scientists estimate that a falcon's binocular vision is about eight times more powerful than a human's. Most of these birds see well in color, too. In addition, they are able to quickly focus their eyes on moving objects while they are also in motion themselves.

Three pairs of eyelids protect a falcon's eyeballs. Scientists often compare the third set to goggles that keep the bird's eyes clean and moist while it is flying. The falcon can still see even when this outer pair of eyelids is shut. Meanwhile, a bony ridge above its eyes offers shade and extra protection from objects such as branches.

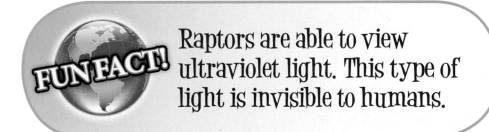

FUN FACT! Raptors are able to view ultraviolet light. This type of light is invisible to humans.

Most falcon species have large eyes.

An Overview of Ears

Falcons do not have external ears like people do. Instead, they have ear holes. These openings are hidden by feathers and positioned behind and underneath a falcon's eyes. Scientists estimate that falcons' sense of hearing is roughly the same as that of human beings. It's possible that they use their ears to locate prey, but most species probably rely more heavily on their eyes.

The forest falcon of Central and South America relies more on its sense of hearing than its sight. This bird lives in tropical rain forests filled with trees and thick plant life. Such growth makes it hard for the rays of the sun to filter downward to the forest floor. As a result, limited light creates challenges for predators that hunt using sight alone. South American forest falcons have adapted to this environment by developing larger ear holes. This provides them with more powerful hearing, which they depend on to track down prey.

A forest falcon's sharp hearing helps it detect noises made by prey.

Breathing Basics

Falcons don't have a remarkable sense of smell. However, they still need the nostrils located along their beak to breathe in oxygen. Their powerful lungs exchange oxygen with carbon dioxide, which is a waste product of **respiration**. Falcons do not breathe out. Instead, air sacs attached to a falcon's lungs release carbon dioxide from its body.

Only certain animals have air sacs. Mammals do not. They rely on their lungs to both breathe in oxygen and force out carbon dioxide. This increases the time it takes for oxygen to spread throughout the body. A one-way airflow has the opposite effect. It keeps falcons breathing steadily even when they suddenly change speed or direction.

So does a small tubercle, or bony bump, inside each of a falcon's nostrils. During sharp dives, birds experience changes in air pressure. Tubercles help falcons adjust to these shifts by slowing the flow of air passing over their nostrils.

A falcon's tubercles prevent too much air from entering the bird's nostrils during a dive.

CHAPTER 3

A Falcon's Life Cycle

A falcon's life span varies from species to species. For example, prairie falcons typically live only a few years in the wild. Meanwhile, peregrines have an average life span of about 13 years, and some have reached nearly twice that age. Yet many of these birds don't even survive their first year of life. This is mainly because they are often injured in falls and crashes while learning how to fly.

Most falcons are solitary animals. They prefer to live alone and tend to be territorial, or protective of their living space. Exceptions include red-throated caracaras, which spend time in groups called casts.

Falcons make cackling, chattering, and wailing noises to communicate. They also croak, squawk, and whine. Depending on the species, certain flight patterns and even changes in skin color are used to communicate as well. Falcons generally use these sounds and displays to signal ownership of their territory and to attract **mates**.

Red-throated caracaras are named for the bright coloring around their mouth and neck.

Raptor Reproduction

Scientists believe that most falcons are monogamous. This means they form mating pairs for life. Falcons **reproduce** once a year. Mating typically occurs between late winter and early summer. Once a male falcon, or tiercel, succeeds in attracting a mate, he becomes responsible for hunting the pair's food. Meanwhile, females remain close to their nesting site.

Females usually lay one to seven eggs at a time. The eggs hatch roughly 28 to 35 days later. During this period, the female falcon sits on top of the eggs to keep them warm. When she takes a break to feed, the tiercel takes a turn caring for them.

Though falcons are fierce hunters, they are often very gentle parents. Scientists have even observed them curling up their feet while near their eggs. This motion helps protect the unborn birds from the adults' sharp talons.

FUN FACT! Every so often, a falcon uses its beak to turn its eggs. This helps ensure that the eggs are heated evenly.

A peregrine falcon keeps careful watch over its eggs.

From Eggs to Adulthood

Baby falcons are called eyases. When they hatch, they look quite different from their parents. They are more lightly colored. They are also covered in down, or soft, fluffy feathers. Mother falcons hardly ever leave their young for the first 7 to 10 days after they are born.

Eyases do not venture outside their nest for one to two months. During this nestling period, they lose their down and grow feathers better suited to flying. The parents hunt prey for their babies. The mother tears the food into smaller pieces that the eyases are able to swallow.

Once they are approximately four to eight weeks old, most falcons fledge, or attempt their first flight. Yet many still require help feeding for several months. By watching their parents hunt, younger falcons eventually become more independent. They are usually ready to have babies of their own when they are between one and three years old.

Eyases are covered in fuzzy feathers that keep them warm but are not very good for flying.

CHAPTER 4

Past and Present Identity

Falcons belong to the Falconidae family. The word *falco* is Latin for "falcon." The term *idae* has Latin and Greek roots and refers to membership within a family of animals.

The earliest species of Falconidae first appeared about 76 million to 55 million years ago. This is when dinosaurs still roamed the earth! Today, scientists group these raptors into one of two subfamilies. Members of the first group, Falconinae, are often simply called falcons. This subfamily is made up of true falcons, falconets, pygmy falcons, and spot-winged falconets.

Peregrines, gyrfalcons, and several species of kestrels are examples of true falcons. Most are medium-sized raptors known for their exceptional sight, flight speed, and hunting abilities. True falcons are found on almost every continent. Meanwhile, falconets, pygmy falcons, and spot-winged falconets exist mainly in Southeast Asia, Africa, and South America. They are among the smallest diurnal raptors.

Like other true falcons, kestrels are fairly small birds.

The Second Subfamily

Polyborinae is the second subfamily of falcons. It features laughing falcons, forest falcons, and five different **genera** of caracaras. Many of these birds live deep in the forests of Central, South, and North America. As a result, they're often harder to study than the Falconinae species.

Based on scientists' observations, it seems that birds within Polyborinae frequently spend time close to the ground. Since they do less speedy diving, they have a few different physical features than members of Falconinae. Some examples include longer legs, a longer tail, and more rounded wings.

In addition, caracaras usually have a bare face. This sometimes causes them to look more like vultures than falcons. Caracaras hunt small birds and mammals, but they are also well-known scavengers. This means that they feed on prey that has already been killed by other animals.

A crested caracara investigates a dead cow while scavenging for food along the ground.

Rethinking Relatives

For a long time, scientists believed that falcons were closely related to hawks and eagles. They noted physical similarities between these predatory birds, including their sharp eyesight and fierce beak and talons. Scientists also acknowledged that one of the biggest differences between them is how they kill prey. Hawks and eagles use their talons, while falcons rely on their beak.

However, experts eventually discovered other important qualities that set these raptors apart. In 2011, they declared that falcons actually have closer family ties to perching birds and parrots. They reached this conclusion by conducting genetic research. Genetics is the study of how certain traits are passed from parents to their young.

In addition to genetic similarities, scientists also pointed out that falcons share various physical features with parrots and passerines. One such passerine is the shrike, a medium-sized perching songbird. Only shrikes and falcons possess a tomial tooth. Like falcons, shrikes use their tomial tooth to quickly kill prey.

Most parrots have very brightly colored feathers.

CHAPTER 5

The Future for Falcons

Falcons and humans share a complicated relationship. For roughly 2,000 years people have trained and used falcons for hunting other animals. Yet certain people view falcons more as pests than helpful hunting partners. For example, some farmers complain that falcons attack and kill their animals.

Unfortunately, human activity has often had a negative impact on these birds. Not all falcons have adapted to life in cities and other developed areas. Cutting down trees and clearing forests have led to habitat loss. Falcons are injured and sometimes even die when they crash into man-made objects such as windmills or power lines.

Also, pesticides have taken a toll on many falcon species. Pesticides are substances used to kill insects. Their chemical makeup has been known to harm other animals, too. During the 1960s and 1970s, several falcon groups suffered from pesticide poisoning.

Falconers wear special gloves to protect their arms while handling birds.

Protecting Remarkable Raptors

Sadly, the Guadalupe caracara and Réunion kestrel are already **extinct**. At present, one species of falcon—the saker falcon—is endangered. This means that it is at very high risk of becoming extinct in the wild. Four other species are listed as vulnerable, or at high risk of extinction. These are the grey falcon, the Mauritius kestrel, the plumbeous forest falcon, and the Seychelles kestrel.

Conservationists offer hope for the future. They educate the public about falcons and how they are affected by human activity. Some scientists hatch eggs in captivity and then release young birds back into the wild. This has helped reintroduce certain species to areas where they had previously grown scarce. Ideally, such efforts will continue to prove successful.

People still have much to learn about falcons. Hopefully these remarkable raptors will grace the skies for many years to come.

The Mauritius kestrel is one of the rarest falcon species.

Words to Know

adapted (uh-DAPT-id) — changed in order to fit a new setting or set of circumstances

carrion (KAR-ee-uhn) — dead animal flesh

conservationists (kon-sur-VAY-shun-ists) — people who work to protect an environment and the living things in it

diurnal (dye-UR-nuhl) — describing an animal that is typically active during the day and asleep at night

environments (en-VYE-ruhn-muhnts) — the natural surroundings of living things, such as the air, land, or sea

extinct (ik-STINGKT) — no longer found alive; known about only through fossils or history

family (FAM-uh-lee) — a group of living things that are related to each other

genera (JEN-ur-uh) — groups of related plants or animals that are larger than a species but smaller than a family

habitats (HAB-uh-tats) — places where an animal or a plant is usually found

mammals (MAM-uhlz) — warm-blooded animals that have hair or fur and usually give birth to live babies; female mammals produce milk to feed their young

mates (MAYTS) — animals that join with other animals to reproduce

metabolism (muh-TAB-uh-liz-uhm) — the rate at which nutrients and energy are used to maintain body functions

migrate (MYE-grate) — to move to another area or climate at a particular time of year

mudflat (MUHD-flat) — a coastal wetland that is alternately covered by water and left bare, depending on the movement of local tides

predatory (PREH-duh-tor-ee) — living by hunting other animals for food

prey (PRAY) — an animal that's hunted by another animal for food

reproduce (ree-pruh-DOOS) — to produce offspring or individuals of the same kind

reptiles (REP-tylz) — cold-blooded animals that crawl across the ground or creep on short legs; most reptiles have backbones and reproduce by laying eggs

respiration (res-pur-AY-shuhn) — the act or process of breathing in and breathing out

savannas (suh-VAN-uhz) — flat, grassy plains with few or no trees; savannas are found in tropical and subtropical areas

species (SPEE-sheez) — one of the groups into which animals and plants of the same genus are divided; members of the same species can mate and have offspring

talons (TAL-uhnz) — the sharp claws of a bird such as an eagle, hawk, or falcon

tundras (TUHN-druhz) — very cold areas of northern Europe, Asia, and Canada where there are no trees and the soil under the surface of the ground is always frozen

Habitat Map

NORTH

AMERICA

PACIFIC

OCEAN

ATLANTIC

SOUTH
AMERICA

Falcon Range

ARCTIC OCEAN

EUROPE

ASIA

AFRICA

PACIFIC OCEAN

OCEAN

INDIAN

OCEAN

AUSTRALIA

Find Out More

Books

De la Bédoyère, Camilla. *100 Things You Should Know About Birds of Prey*. Broomall, PA: Mason Crest Publishers, 2011.

Lunis, Natalie. *Peregrine Falcon: Dive, Dive, Dive!* New York: Bearport Publishing Company, Inc., 2011.

Povey, Karen D. *Falcons*. Farmington Hills, MI: KidHaven Press, 2005.

Visit this Scholastic Web site for more information on falcons:
www.factsfornow.scholastic.com
Enter the keyword **Falcons**

Index

Page numbers in *italics* indicate a photograph or map.

adaptations, 9, 22, 38
adulthood, 30
air sacs, 25

babies. *See* eyases.
beaks, 6, 10, 18, *19*, 29, 37
binocular vision, 21
breathing, *24*, 25

caracaras, *16*, 17, 26, *27*, 34, *35*, 41
carrion, 13
colors, 10, 21, 26, *27*, 30, *36*
communication, 26
conservation, 41

digestion, 13, 18
diurnal raptors, 6, 13, 33
diving, 6, 14, 17, *24*, 25, 34

ears, 22, *23*
eating, 13, 18
eggs, *28*, 29, 41
endangered species, 41
eyases, 30, *31*
eyes, 10, *20*, 21, 22, 37

falconets, 33
farming, 9, 38
feathers, 10, 14, 17, 22, 30, *31*, *36*
feet, 10, 17, 29
females, *11*, 29, 30

fledging, 30
flying, 13, 14, *15*, 21, 26, 30, 33, 38
food. *See* prey.
forest falcons, 22, *23*, 34, 41

genetics, 37
gyrfalcons, 10, *10*, *11*, 33

habitats, 6, 9, 22, 33, 34, 38
hatching, 29, 30, 41
hearing, 22, *23*
hunting, 6, *7*, 13, 17, 18, 21, 22, 29, 30, 33, 34, 38

injuries, 14, 26, 38

keels, 14
kestrels, 10, *10*, *32*, 33, *40*, 41

legs, *16*, 17, 34
life spans, 26
lungs, 25

males. *See* tiercels.
mating, 26, 29
metabolism, 13
migration, 9
muscles, 14, 17

necks, 14, *27*
nests, *8*, 9, 29, 30

(Index continued)

nostrils, *24*, 25

parrots, *36*, 37
passerines, 37
people, 21, 38, *39*, 41
peregrine falcons, 6, 9, 14, 26, *28*, 33
pesticides, 38
predators, 13
prey, 6, *7*, 9, *12*, 13, 14, 17, 18, *19*, 21,
    22, 30, 34, *35*, 37, 38

red-throated caracaras, 26, *27*
Réunion kestrels, 41

scavenging, 34, *35*
scrapes, 9, 17
Seychelles kestrels, 10, *10*, 41
shrikes, 37
sizes, 10, *10*, *11*, *32*, 33

solitude, 26
species, 9, 10, 13, 17, 22, 26, 33, 34,
    38, 41
speeds, 6, 14, 33
stomachs, 13

tails, 14, 34
talons, 6, 10, 17, 29, 37
territories, 26
tiercels, 29, 30
toes, 10, 17
tomial teeth, 18, 37
true falcons, *32*, 33
tubercles, *24*, 25

weight, 10
wings, 14, 34
wingspans, 10, *10*

About the Author

Katie Marsico is the author of more than 150 children's books. She enjoyed learning about falcons and spotted quite a few while writing about them during her vacation in southwestern Florida.